SECRETS ON FIBONACCI TRADING

Mastering Fibonacci Techniques In Less Than 3 Days

FRANK MILLER

TABLE OF CONTENTS

FOREWORD

Why are you still losing money in trading? Why, after few years of active trading, are you not making profit despite the fact that you have read dozen of trading books by professionals? I am quite sure I know the answers to these questions. Just like many unsuccessful traders and investors, you are using the wrong tools.

It may sound ridiculous but think about it. Most books are about lagging indicators, such as oscillators and moving averages. You build your trading plan around those tools but, with time, the contents of your trading account are shrinking because of losses. The reason for this will be discussed in the next part.

The Fibonacci technique is commonly used by professional traders around the world. Also, people who trade for a living have built their trading plans basing on Fibonacci numbers. My knowledge has been built upon years of looking for the best trading tools and the contact I have had with many professionals.

A few years back, when I switched from trading with lagging indicators to the Fibonacci technique, my results have improved. When I added a proper money management to my trading, my results have improved even more. Now, I am a profitable trader and I can show you the path to achieving this.

But let us make one thing straight right at the beginning of this book. I am not selling you a magic formula or system which makes money on every day basis. I am not a con-artist who is trying to sell you a pack of 5 DVDs for 500$ or even 999$ together with a proven system that makes 300% profit in one year. Such systems do not exist. Of course, there is automated trading, but in this case the system has to be optimized. Markets are constantly changing, so are optimization parameters. You may buy a system which has worked well on historical data, but suddenly starts losing money. Be aware of this!

In this e-book I want to show you what Fibonacci trading is all about and teach you how to use it. You will learn which trigger works best and when is the right time to exit. There is an important chapter about money management, because, without capital preservation, you are doomed to failure. I will teach you when and how to enter a trade and when to exit it.

But remember – you are responsible for your trading results. I show you these great tools, teach you how to manage your money, but unless you follow basic rules presented in this book, you will not be able to succeed.

I assume that you have some basic knowledge of technical analysis. In order to understand concepts from this e-book, you should know what candle is, how support and resistance works, how basic candle formations looks like. These are basic concepts, and since this is an e-book about trading according to Fibonacci, I will not describe them in detail. If you do not know these tools, browse the Internet for more information first and then come back and finish reading this book.

I am sure you will achieve success in trading. It takes some time to learn and understand Fibonacci, but it pays off. I have tried to put many examples into this book, with the hope of helping you to gain the best understanding of an excellent tool in trading platform.

CHAPTER 1: INTRODUCTION

In Chapter 1 you will learn:

- What Fibonacci numbers are
- What the main difference between trading with classic technical analysis tools and Fibonacci tools is
- What the Fibonacci ratio is

Why is "Buy and hold" not that great?

Many people still believe in old concepts of trading. Some are convinced that buy and hold is the best way to make money. They want to be like Warren Buffet. They read about investing in value. They believe that buying and holding shares of some good company is the smartest way to earn money. They think that by this way they will beat short-term trading gamblers. In crisis and recession as we have today, it doesn't really matter if a company is that great. In panic, people very often sell off all their assets. They withdraw money from invest funds, so the funds have to sell their shares, even those of good companies.

Just look at the chart of S&P500. If you bought long contract at this index in 2001, after 10 years your profit would oscillate around zero dollars!

1.1.   *S&P500 futures, weekly chart, 1999 - 2012*

This could be money for your retirement, college fund for your kids or simply your savings. No profit here. S&P500 includes 500 biggest companies in the USA. Even if you have invested in some of them, the chances are that you have made no profit.

Trend following is simple, but…

OK, if not buy and hold, then maybe trend following? You constantly hear:

- Trend is your friend
- Trend following is the best way to make money in the market
- Follow the trend and never look back

… and so on, and so forth. However, the problem is that nowadays markets tend to move very fast, especially when they fall. What is the best tool to follow trends? Where should I enter and close position? Is it the end of a move or will be there a continuation?

In many cases, trend following investors try to make decisions based on moving averages and oscillators.

When the market is oversold, you should go long, and then follow the trend and exit on the signal that the market is overbought. Sounds pretty easy, doesn't it? So, why are the majority of investors losing money?

The main difference on example

Let's have a look at the same trade.

The first investor makes his decisions basing on the trend following system. He is using the Stochastic oscillator, and two simple moving averages (later I will be using the MA shortcut) – 10 and 20 period long. The buy signal is when Stochastic is oversold, and there is a cross of 10 MA over 20 MA. The exit signal is when 10 MA is back below 20 MA. Let's take a look at the below chart:

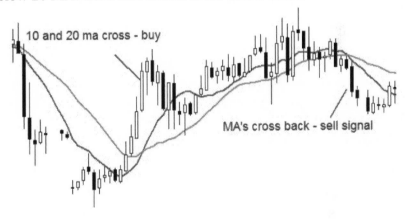

10 and 20 ma cross - buy

MA's cross back - sell signal

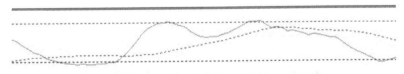

1.2.   *Late entry and exit based on lagging indicators*

The entry point was very late because of the fast move of price and the late cross of MAs. The exit signal was also very late.

The other trader is using the Fibonacci technique. He chooses swing, draws the Fibonacci retracement levels and waits for an entry signal at correction. When the signal occurs, he pulls the trigger and enters the trade. He draws the Fibonacci extensions level to get the idea of when to close the trade. After a while, his target is achieved and he exits the trade. Please refer the following chart:

1.3.   *Fibonacci trader and his point of view at this same trade.*

Naturally, both examples are simplified, so that you can see the difference more clearly. Don't worry if you don't understand the second example. When you finish this e-book, this will be an easy thing for you to do. For the time being, just follow the decision process of the two traders.

Mind when the first trader made his decision to enter the trade. Look when he closed it. It was very late to take profit.

And now take a close look at the second trader. Again, it is the same chart, same day, but the second trader is using different tools. Notice that his enter and exit decisions were made long before the first trader's! He made more money on the same trade, and exit when the first trader was still hoping for continuation of the trend.

This is the main difference between traders using lagging indicators and those using leading indicators.

Lagging indicators are based on prices from the past. It may be a price that was open, close, low, high, but a price from the past in all cases. It does not matter if you are using MACD, moving averages, RSI, CCI or other oscillators. They all are lagging indicators and they give signal after it took place, like we could see in the first example.

The Fibonacci tool, on the other hand, is a tool belonging to leading oscillators. These give you support and resistance levels for the price before it even gets there. You should decide or use others tools to take the most probable signal. There is a whole chapter about choosing best signals later on in the e-book, so you will understand it better. Using the leading indicator let the second trader get ahead of the rest people using lagging indicators. This is the main reason why so many investors are not profitable. Professionals use leading indicators to be the first to enter and exit the trade.

Soon enough you will join this group!

Where do Fibonacci numbers come from?

I will try to make the Fibonacci topic simple and comprehensive. In a moment, we will focus on trading, but some basic topics have to be explained. Try to understand them well. Do not worry; it is not as complicated as you think!

Leonardo Pisano Bigollo (born around 1170 in Italy), also known as Leonardo Fibonacci, introduced the Fibonacci sequence to the western world in his book *Liber Abaci*. What is interesting, this sequence was known to Indian mathematicians back in six century.

The Fibonacci sequence is present in many different areas, such as mathematics, nature (spirals of shells or tree branches) and, of course, in trading! If you are interested in other areas that you can find this, you should read a publication about Fibonacci numbers.

Firstly, a few words about Fibonacci numbers. What are they, anyway?

Fibonacci numbers are the sequence of numbers starting as follows: 0, 1, 1, 2, 3, 5, 8, 13, 21, 34, 55, 89, 144, 233, 337, 610, 987...

Each number is a sum of two previous numbers (two to the left).

Look at number 3. It is the sum of number 2 and number 1, because 2 and 1 are to the left of 3.

The two numbers to the left of 34 are 21 and 13. So, we add 21 to 13 and the result is 34.

This is the answer to where Fibonacci numbers came from. Each Fibonacci number has its own place in the sequence. The sequence is the base to calculating other Fibonacci numbers, such as ratio or extension.

What is the Fibonacci retracement and ratio?

Based on the sequence, we can calculate the ratio. The **Fibonacci ratio is counted by dividing a number by the number that follows it in the sequence**. Let's take a look at some examples:

$5/8=0.625$

$13/21=0.619$

$89/144=0.618$

The last ratio listed: 61.8% is the most important ratio and is often called the golden ratio. But there are more ratios, as you have noticed. Where do the other ratios come from? The answer is simple: it is the result of dividing a number standing two, three and four places to the right.

For instance, two places to the right from 8 there is 21:

$8/21=0.38$

Three places from 8 there is 33:

$8/33=0.24$

Here we have them – the most important ratios: 23.6%, 38.2%, 61.8%.

A ratio is also called a retracement level. It is because there is a chance that a price will stop and reverse at one of those levels.

Traders like to use a few levels more, so the list of most popular full retracement levels is as follows:

23.6%, 38.2%, 50%, 61.8%, 78%

The 50% retracement level does not come from the Fibonacci sequence, but it's an important level. Traders tend to react when a price is near half of the previous swing, so they added it to retracement levels.

Price behavior

Before we learn more about the Fibonacci retracements, let's focus on price behavior for a minute.

Let's start from one tricky question and the basics of price behavior. In which direction can price move? You will probably answer: up and down. This answer is correct, there is a "but" though. What if there is no main trend? If there is no strong trend, the price will probably move sideways. Statistics say that the price is moving about 30% of time in a trend and rest of this time it is moving in a range. Why is moving in a range such a bad thing? It is because there is no clear direction and the price moves up and down, so it is very hard to make money in this kind of movement. Have a look at the chart below, is it the way you would like to trade in?

1.4.   *Range market example.*

No, it is not. It is a very tough market to stay profitable in. Unless you like to trade in a range, you should avoid this kind of market. The best way is to wait until it is over and then start to make money when the trend is back.

Price can be trending up, down or move sideways. Of course, we look for investment opportunities in an up and down trend, trying to avoid investing when there is no clear direction.

Let's assume that we have identified an uptrend. Does the price go up all the time? No, it makes higher highs and higher lows. This is a sign for us that there is an uptrend. It may look similar to the example below:

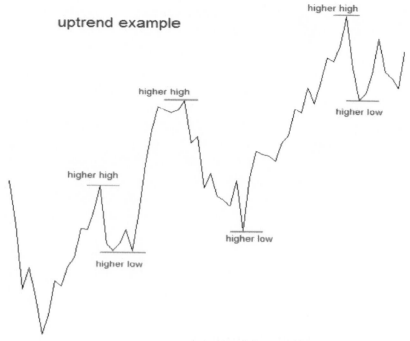

1.5.   *An uptrend and higher highs.*

It is similar with the downtrend. The price makes lower highs and lower lows. Again, look at chart below and you should understand it right away:

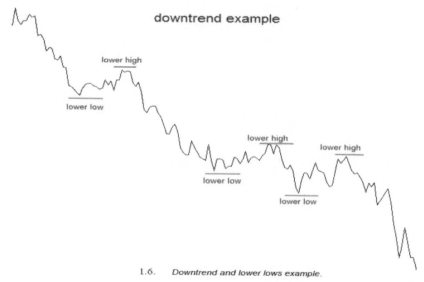

1.6.   *Downtrend and lower lows example.*

Can you see the clear sequence of this move? There is certain noise around it, but you should be able to spot significant highs and lows.

This behavior gives us important information. First of all, we are able to identify the current trend. When we are able to see the higher highs, we can draw the Fibonacci retracement levels. Identification of the turning points (higher highs and higher lows or lower highs and lower lows) is necessary to draw retracement correctly. You can read how to draw it in a little while.

Remember: in some unusual cases the price will go straight up or down. This happens mostly when some unexpected news is causing panic or euphoria among investors. It looks promising on a chart, but trading this is very hard. You have to take your position early; otherwise, later your entry point will be very risky.

1.7. *Strong drop and very dangerous situation.*

What is the aim of this e-book?

Before you "make your hands dirty" with trading, I want to tell you about the main aim of this e-book and the idea behind it.

There are some good books about Fibonacci numbers and using them in trading. There are also some courses which you can buy for as little as 799$ (sic!) and you can learn from them about the magic system based on the mystic Fibonacci tools.

There is no such a thing! (I know that I am repeating myself already, but it is important.) There is you and there is the market. Many have failed in trying to make a fortune on trading, so you have to be careful and respect the market. There is no magic trick or system, there is a lot of hard work and a lot of things you have to learn. You should learn the best techniques that will give you advantage.

This is the aim of this e-book. I am convinced that the Fibonacci tools are your edge in trading. You have to get to know them and use them well to be successful. It does not matter if you trade stocks, Forex or bonds. You will find the Fibonacci ratios there.

I focus mainly on the Fibonacci retracement and extension and I will show you how to enter and exit the trade at best moments. There is also a chapter about money management. It is also a very important part of trading.

I will only mention other Fibonacci tools like time zones, arc or fan. Is it because they are not useful? No, but, in my opinion, they are not the most important ones. I wanted to write an e-book for traders who are beginners and at the intermediate level regarding their trading skills. I know from my experience that using all the tools at the same time can do more bad than good. The masters in using the retracement and extension lines, learn how to manage their position, where to put stop losses and this makes them better traders. That is the main goal for me: to teach you the best techniques and give you solid background in the Fibonacci trading.

Now, as we understand each other better, let's move on to more advanced topics.

CHAPTER 2: FIBONACCI RETRACEMENT LEVELS

In the previous chapter, you have learned about the most popular retracement levels (23.6%, 38.2%, 50%, 61.8%, 78%). Now, it is time to learn how to draw them and how you can use them in your trading.

How to draw the retracement levels? It is easy like ABC

So far, we have learned that it is very rare for a price to move in one direction for a longer time. Surely, when there is panic or euphoria on the market because of some big news, prices may skyrocket and it is hard to enter the trade.

In most cases though, the price moves in zigzag shapes. Some traders call it waves, and there is a scientific concept called Elliott wave theory. But for us it is important to know the nature of these moves. First, we need to identify a swing move that is a move from point A to point B. We know already that after the main swing there should be a correction in the opposite direction to point C. When we see a move from point A to B, we wait for a move down (correction) to point C. Point C should be located between points A and B. On a chart illustrating an uptrend it may look like this:

2.1. An ABC move example.

It is not always so easy to identify points A, B, and C, but it gets easier with time and experience. When we are sure that we have found the ABC move, we can draw a Fibonacci retracement with a tool from our chart software. We start from the low of swing to the high, so from point A to point B.

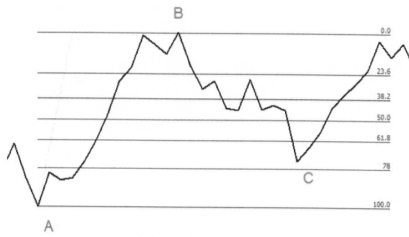

2.2. Drawing retracement lines from the low to the high (A to B).

If you use candle charts, you should draw from the low of the shadow (or peak) of a candle to the high of a candle. Please, notice that you get much more accurate results when you apply the retracement levels to your candle chart. Compare it with the results from the above chart.

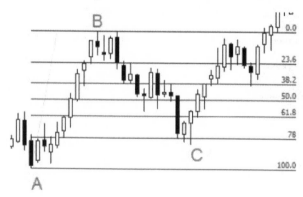

2.3. Drawing retracement lines from the low of the shadow to the high of a candle.

How do you know if you have chosen the right top and bottom? It is a little bit like art and comes with time. At times, when you have two bottoms nearby, even if you have selected the wrong one, it is not going to change the position of the retracement levels so much. Just practice on the price history.

Should the price touch the retracement levels?

This is always a problem for new investors. They think that the retracement to point C is only valid when the price touches down this level. They are wrong. Fibonacci retracements are a great tool, but there is no 100% accuracy. Sometimes the price closes near the retracement level and it can be still a valid move. Just look at the example below.

Example

In a downtrend, there was a correction up. The price looked as if it would move up to 50% retracement level, but it did not happen.

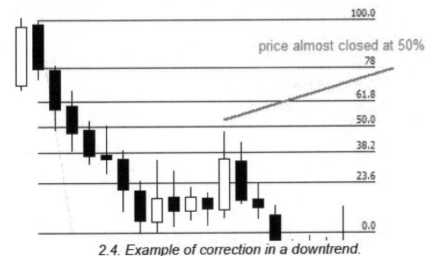

2.4. Example of correction in a downtrend.

The result was that both candles closed below the 38% level. Still, it is a valid correction to point C, and then the price moved back to a downtrend. Try to pay attention to this. On numerous occasions the price will almost touch your retracement level, which is great. However, be aware that sometimes the price only draws near that level, and still trading is worth continuing.

What retracement levels should I use?

It is very confusing at the beginning, because there are many Fibonacci retracement levels and some people use only specific ones, while others like to draw all the retracements. My advice is to try to use the standard levels. Over time, when you gain more experience, you will decide which the most important ones are and which ones you prefer to use.

So, which levels should you start with?

- **23.6%**
- **38.2%**
- **50%**
- **61.8%**
- **78%.**

Why use the 50%? It is not a Fibonacci retracement, but still an important level (half way up or down), so traders like to keep this retracement level together with other proper levels. Stick to these levels and it should be enough to trade well when it comes to price correction.

I have my retracement lines, when should I open a trade?

Now you know how to draw the retracement lines. Thanks to them you can enter a trade with a better price, which is always a good thing.

But when should you enter a trade?

That is the biggest challenge after drawing the right retracements levels. You can find a more specific information about entering a trade in Part 5. Before you read that part, it is important that you understand the options you have when the price is nears the retracement line.

After drawing the retracement levels, you should decide when you want to open your position. You have three options to choose from, but before further explanation, check the chart below.

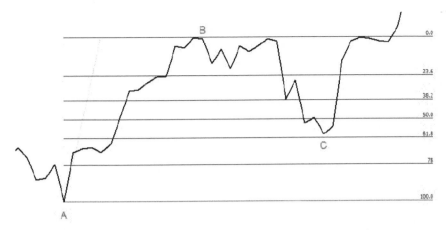

2.5. Line chart and correction to the point C – example.

I do not want to complicate things too much, so I have used a line chart, but in real trading, try to use a candlestick chart:

We have confirmed that the main trend is strong and is up. After a swing move from A to B, there was a strong correction, so we have drawn the retracement levels. We are waiting to take a long position, because the main trend is up.

Now we have three options of doing this.

Option 1

You are willing to take bigger risk in turn for a possible bigger return. When the price (almost) reaches the 61.8% retracement, you go long at this level or a little bit above it. This level is very popular among traders, so, very often, at least for a moment, the price stops here and bounces back.

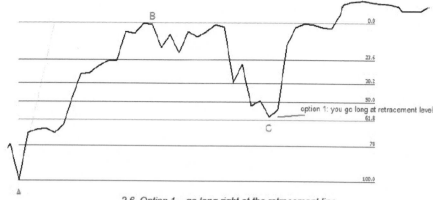

You can take the same action at 50% or 38.2% if you think that the correction ends and there is your point C.

Remember, this may not be a bounce to new highs. You do not have the knowledge about it at the time of trading. Having seen the right side of the chart and you know that in that case the correction ended on the 61.8% level. In real life, when you choose this option, you never know if the correction really ended at point C or it was just a false move. But if you are right, your possible profit can be very big.

Option 2

The second option is when you wait and watch how the price reacts towards the retracement levels. If you see that 61.8% is probably the retracement which a bounce back may occur from, you are ready to take a long position. But unlike the first case, you wait for another confirmation. It could be many things, such as a confirmation from an oscillator or moving averages – simply something that is written in your trading plan. When there is a confirmation signal, you go long. Of course, confirmation signals are not always 100% correct, but in that case you have lower chance of failure. This, in my opinion, is a better way to enter trades. The ratio between risk and possible profit is very good. In this example, the trader decided that the signal will be a close of price above resistance.

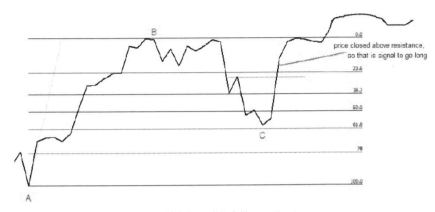

2.7. Entry after signal to go long.

As I have mentioned, you have to decide and test yourself what signal works best for you.

Option 3

In the third case you wait until the price breaks above the recent high (the one you have used to draw your retracement levels - point B). There is a good chance that the move will continue. This way of trading is the safest one, but your possible profit is the smallest.

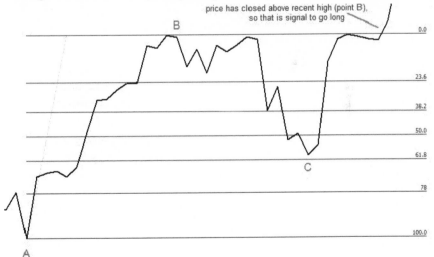

2.8. Entry after price breakout.

Personally, I trade according to the third scenario very often. The reason for this is simple – there may be a big mess near retracement level and I cannot get a confirmation signal. I simply wait for the break above point B and go long at this point.

Which way is the best for you? It is your decision. It depends greatly on your trading skills and mental strength. How much risk are you willing to take? Do you have good and working confirmation signals? You should try all the three ways and decide which one you like the most and can make most money with.

You do not buy blindly at the top anymore. Now you have the knowledge and you wait for the correction to buy for a better (lower) price. Of course, your aim is not to catch the bottom, because it is very hard to do, but if you buy after the correction ends, you are ahead of many others investors.

Where to put stops?

The Fibonacci retracements are great when it comes to placing stop losses. Let's assume that you have a long position opened after a correction to point C. Where should you place the stop loss order? I like to put it below point A, that is, below the place where the swing move started. If the price moves back down below point A, there is probably something wrong with the trend strength.

Below, I marked 3 possible places where you can place your stop loss order in such a case:

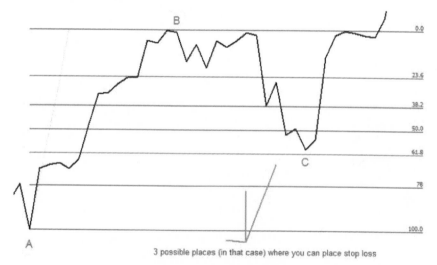

3 possible places (in that case) where you can place stop loss

2.9. Possible places where you can put your stop losses.

It all depends on how aggressive you want to trade. Sometimes I place stop loss just below the 78% retracement line. If you want to place a tide stop loss, you place it below the retracement that you think is your point C.

The good thing is that, over time, you will understand the behavior of the price better and you will be able to place the stop losses in better places.

There is more about the topic in Part 5, where entering a trade is discussed in detail.

The retracement and trend lines

Sometimes the price trends very nicely and it is easy to see the trend line. In such a case there is a strong chance that when it comes to a correction, it will end at a Fibonacci retracement level closest to the trend line.

Fibonacci works great on the trending markets, so it is a good idea to combine these tools. First, you have to draw a trend line.

2.10. Price respecting a trend line – example.

Let's assume you are waiting for a retest of this line. In the meantime, you can also draw the Fibonacci retracement levels from a low to high swing.

2.11. Looking for the best entry point – example.

The correction ended at the 61.8 retracement level and the price touched the trend line. As it turned out, it was a great point to enter the trade.

You can play this scenario by entering the near retracement level and trend line. You put your stop loss below the trend line, but not too far from it. With a strong trend in place, you assume it is a low-risk entry.

It does not always work this well, but sometimes it does. You have to be very watchful about these kinds of price behavior, because these are good points to enter a trade. The potential risk of loss is small and the potential profit is big.

The Fibonacci retracement and support

Another great way to predict where the price move might end is combining the retracement lines with support levels. It is very simple to do. First, you have to check if there is any important support/resistance level. We look for a few types of support. It may be support from previous important highs, like in the example below:

2.12. Break above resistance line – now we can look for retracement level!

Let's say that we want to take a long position after a break above this resistance (so we look for a trade in the area near the right side of the chart). On the lower time frame we can spot swing and correction very fast, down to the 61.8% retracement. If you take a closer look, the correction ended almost exactly at the blue line, which now acted as support (because before the price had closed above that line).

2.13. Closer look at the same situation (from 2.12.) with retracement lines.

Some traders probably took long positions only because price moved back to the support (blue) line. But you know, with your knowledge about Fibonacci, that when an important support line is in the same area as the retracement level, then it is a trade you should consider to take, because there is a much better chance of success.

Another great way to look for support is to combine the retracement levels with moving averages. You probably know that some popular averages work well as support and resistance.

What are these moving averages? They are: 10, 20, 50, 100 and 200 periods long.

Some traders may say that there are more important averages, but this is something you should decide basing on your trading style. From the above set of averages, the most important are the longest ones: 50, 100 and 200. When the price moves back to 200 MA, there is a chance it will find a support there. If you can connect this level with the Fibonacci retracement, you have a potential good entry point.

Below there is a 4 hour chart of S&P500. You can see that the price is above the 50 moving average. After a swing, there is a correction down to that moving average and the 50% retracement level which is in the same place. This is obviously a good point to look for an entry.

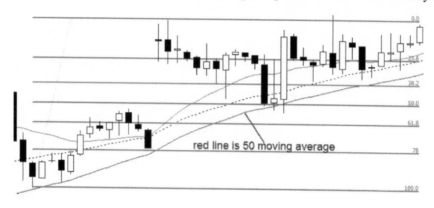

2.14. Good entry point example – 50 MA and 50% retracement line are working together as a strong support.

Take a good look at this combination, because on numerous occasions, this is a good point to enter the trade. Not all traders use the Fibonacci retracement for an entry. Some traders tend to enter or reenter a trade at a moving average, because they know that this is good support. You should join this group, but only when you have another confirmation from the Fibonacci retracement.

CHAPTER 3: FIBONACCI PROJECTIONS

In this part you will learn about the Fibonacci projections and how you can use them to choose your exit point. This is another great tool which can make you a very effective trader.

When do you earn money?

There are two similar tools to project where the price move can end:

- The Fibonacci Extension
- The Fibonacci Expansion

It is confusing at the beginning, but I am going to explain the main differences so you can have good understanding of the subject matter.

Why are the Fibonacci projections so important?

I have seen many cases when people opened the trade at the right moment, for the next few hours or even days the trade was profitable, but they hesitated to close it and ended up with a loss.

The most important thing to remember is that you earn money when you close the trade and book profit from it! If your position was opened two days ago and it is profitable then good for you. But until you close the trade and take the profit, it is virtual profit. It changes all the time. There might be some big news, the price will move against you and in a couple of minutes you will be counting how big your loss is.

This is the reason why closing trades is so important in trading. For me, closing trades is far more important than opening them. Even a poorly executed trade can turn out to be profitable if you exit at the right moment. But when is it the right time and place to take the profit?

The Fibonacci projection is very helpful in solving this problem and I am sure you are going to enjoy it.

Tool 1: The Fibonacci expansion

Let's start with the Fibonacci Expansion, which is based on three points. To draw it we have to identify the swing and correction. Yes, it is exactly like it was with the retracements and looking for points A, B and C. We use the same ABC points. As you remember, we have to identify the swing and correction. Points A and B are marked at the swing ends, C is at the point where the correction ended.

How to draw the expansion levels?

In Metatrader, from the top menu select Insert → Fibonacci → Expansion. Run a trend line from point A to point B.

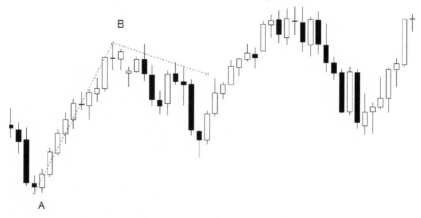

3.1. First step in drawing expansion levels.

Next, you have to click on the end of the second line and move it to point C – where the correction ends.

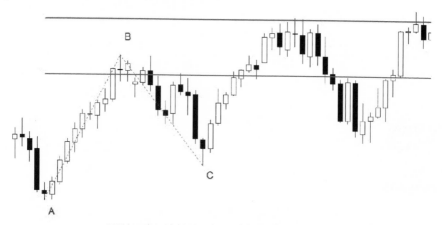

3.2. Next step – moving the end of second line to the point C.

Now you have the possible levels where the move may end or stop for a while. The three most popular are: 61.8; 100 and 161.8. According to this example, it worked very well:

3.3. Expansion lines worked very well – 161.8% was a strong resistance.

The move stopped at two points: the 100 and 161.8 expansion.

How is it calculated?

The expansion levels are drawn from point C:

- Target 61.8 is **0.618** *times* of the distance between **Points A and B**
- Target 100 is **1.000** *times* of the distance between **Points A and B**
- Target 161.8 is **1.618** *times* of the distance between **Points A and B**

That is why in the above example the first target (61.8) is below point B. The correction was deep. The 61.8 target from point C ended below point B. Why? Because there ended the 0.618 distance between A and B.

In another example we will try to find the expansion in a down trend. First, we need to make sure that the down trend is strong, and then we wait for a swing AB and a correction to C.

We start from drawing the expansion from A to B:

3.4. Looking for expansion lines in a downtrend – first step.

Next, we move the second line to point C (where the correction ended):

3.5. Looking for expansion lines – second step.

The expansion levels are now drawn correctly. In this example the price moved down to the 161.8 expansion, but as you can see after the next correction, the down trend has continued. It was a great opportunity to use the expansion levels on the next waves of that move.

3.6. The end result showed on broader view – again 161.8% was a good target.

It gets easier when you practice it yourself. Remember, you have all this historical data to practice with!

Tool 2: the Fibonacci extension

The Fibonacci extension is based on the first move (A to B). Point C is not used for calculation here.

The extension levels are calculated basing on the distance between points A and B. The levels are drawn from point B.

For example, the 138.2% extension level equals the 38.2% distance between A and B, which is drawn from point B. Look closely at the chart below, where I marked the distance:

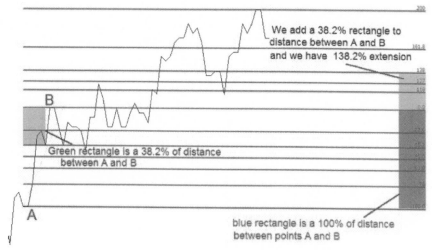

B

Green rectangle is a 38.2% of distance
between A and B

A

We add a 38.2% rectangle to
distance between A and B
and we have 138.2% extension

blue rectangle is a 100% of distance
between points A and B

3.7. The chart shows how Fibonacci extension is calculated.

For the 161.8% extension line we take the 61.8% distance between A and B and add it to point B.

Now you can see that point C (where the correction ends) does not matter in the calculation. We only care about the swing from A to B and this is our base to calculate the extension lines.

It may seem that this method is less accurate, because for the expansion we use 3 points. The truth is that it is also very accurate despite differences in calculation. Personally, this is my favorite way to look for the price projection and later in this e-book I will mostly use this method.

Before we go further and learn more about the extensions, you may want to add them on your Meta-trader chart. Look for instructions at the end of the e-book.

This way you will be able to draw the retracement and extension at the same time! It is handy and saves you a lot of time.

The Fibonacci extension in practice

In the example below you should be able to find points A and B. We can use them to draw the retracement levels as you remember from the previous chapter.

3.8. Drawing extension lines – first you should find AB swing.

In this case we do not pay attention to where exactly the correction ends. Point C will be somewhere between A and B, but in order to calculate the extension we need only A and B. This is what happens next:

3.9. The whole move and stop at 127% extension line.

The correction ended at the 78% retracement level and the price went down to the 127% extension line. It closed almost exactly at this level and right after we noticed a very strong bounce up.

In another example we can also spot a correction down to the 78% retracement. From that point, buyers showed up and the price moved up strong up to the 138% extension where it stopped for a while. Later the price moved up to the 161.8% extension which was a very strong resistance for a long time.

Actually, the price did not move above that level and sellers took control.

3.9. Extension lines in an uptrend – example.

Later I will present more examples of trades and signal confirmations. For now, it is important for you to understand the difference between the Fibonacci extension and expansion.

Expansion -> 3 points (ABC) to calculate the expansion levels

Extension -> 2 points (AB) to calculate the extension levels

Both tools are great. You can plan your exit points and book profits thanks to them. My favorite one is the Fibonacci extension, so in the next trade examples I focus mostly on that tool. If you like the Fibonacci expansion better, feel free to try it out and build your own trading plan on it. The expansion is used by many traders as well, so maybe it is the right tool for you?

Which extension levels are most important?

There are so many projection levels that you might be confused which ones are the best in practice. To tell the truth, there is no single rule, such as "always close at the extension of 138%".

Some traders like to draw only a few levels on their charts to keep things clean, but they are aware of the fact that the price might stop at other levels.

The most common extension levels are: 127%, 138.2%, 161.8%, 261.8%.

Other levels, such as 118%, 150% or 200% are also important and can stop the price action. Over time, you will decide on your own if it is a good idea to keep them all on the chart or only a few. For now, you may stick to the most common extension levels.

It is all about probability

It is important to learn to watch closely how the price reacts with the projection levels.

You do not know in advance where the price will stop. The projection levels are only levels where there is a POSSIBILITY that the price may stop.

It also does not mean that the move will definitely end at the projection level. Sometimes the price stops for a while, and later, if the trend is strong, the move continues. In other cases the move will end at the price projection and it may even be the end of the current trend. That is why you should learn how to watch for the price reaction with the projection levels and to your signals.

Still, you are in a much better situation than other traders. You know in advance the possible levels where the price may stop. You will learn in Part 6 how to use it to your advantage.

CHAPTER 4: FIBONACCI CONVERGENCE

You may use the Fibonacci convergence to find very strong resistance or support. This is very helpful in planning the size of your position, the place of stop loss and the whole action plan.

The convergence can be very useful, but for new traders it is hard to use. It is not that complicated, which I will try to show in this chapter.

Before trading with the Fibonacci convergence you should feel comfortable with using the Fibonacci retracement and extension levels. You should be able to easily choose the price swings to draw them. If you are not that experienced, do not worry! Just read this chapter or skip it and return to study it later when you will have more experience in using the retracement and extension.

At the beginning I wrote that the price moves in a zigzag formation. I showed you how you can choose the swing to draw the Fibonacci retracement or extension. Trends are built upon many different swings. The convergence is a situation when you draw the Fibonacci retracement lines for more than one swing and when some of the levels are close to each other.

In the example below the price moves up making many swings. There are a couple good points to choose to draw the Fibonacci retracement. Which one would you choose?

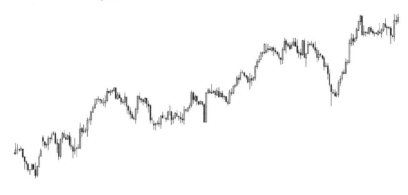

4.1. Clean uptrend and many swings to choose from.

The one below is very easy to spot, so of course we can use this low and high and draw the retracement levels:

4.2. First possible swing where we can draw retracement lines.

We can also use high and low from a bigger move, where the price moved back to the 38.2% retracement line. This is the same chart as the one above:

4.3. Another possible swing to choose.

When we put these two retracement levels together, we will see that some of them are very close to each other:

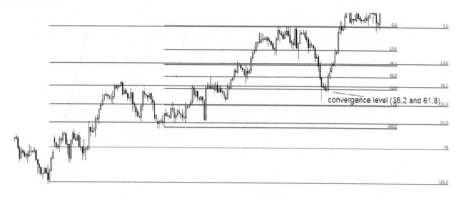

4.4. Putting retracement lines for different swing together.

You can notice that the first convergence level was 38.2 (red) and 23.6 (blue), but the price did not stop there. The second level of convergence was at 61.8 (red) and 38.2 (blue). The price found strong support and from that point the uptrend continued.

CHAPTER 5: IDEAL TIME TO ENTER A TRADE

You have knowledge how the retracement works and what convergence is. In this part I will show you my favorite way to open positions.

When to enter – my favorite system

There are many different ways you can enter a trade with the Fibonacci tools. Now I am going to introduce the safest option which works very well for me for a long time. This is also the option commonly used by many professional traders.

The game plan

The main idea is to buy when the correction ends and there is a breakout. We are looking look for a place where we there is the best chance to enter at the right moment and into right direction. The place is a break above a recent high in an uptrend or below a recent low in a downtrend.

In theory, it should look like in the picture below:

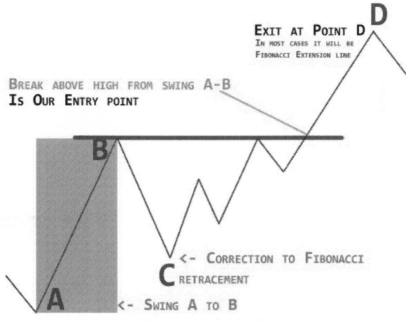

5.1. Looking for a trade in safe scenario.

The game plan is simple.

1. Identify the main trend (you can read the instruction in Part 7). You should know what the main trend is and in which direction you will be looking to enter a trade.
2. Identify the low-high/high-low swing. Find the swing which you will draw the retracement and extension lines for.
3. Wait for the end of the correction to part C. Let other traders play between the retracement lines. Just be ready and wait to enter the position.
4. Wait for the breakout above the high from swing A-B (to go long) or below the low from swing A-B (to go short).
5. Wait until the price moves to the extension line and closes the position at point D.

The main difference between a Fibonacci trader and an ordinary trader

This game plan is simple. You may have noticed that many other traders are taking positions at breakouts, because chances that the move will continue in the main trend direction are the best.

But there is one huge difference between a Fibonacci trader and an ordinary trader. The latter is not sure when he should close the trade. He has opened the position at the right time (at the breakout), but he has no clue where to close it. He has some exit signals, but he is usually late with his exit decision.

A Fibonacci trader is able to get the most part of move from the moment of breakout. With the Fibonacci extension tool he can, on many occasions, exit almost exactly at the end of the move (it is not the goal of this strategy, but it will happen to you many times).

In this scenario you take less risk. When the price closes above a recent high, there is a strong chance there will be a continuation of the up movement.

Your exit point will be on one of the extension lines (more about closing positions in the next part). Your goal is to catch most of the move between 100% and the extension line, so between 100% and 127% or 138.2% or 161.8% etc.

Examples

Below there is a 4-hour chart of GBP/USD. From a higher time frame we know that the main trend is up. There is a deep correction (down to the 61.8% level, C point). At this point we are still waiting for a breakout. After a while, there is our breakout above point B (recent high). The green field marks out our potential profit zone (it could get even higher), that is everything between point B and the extension lines.

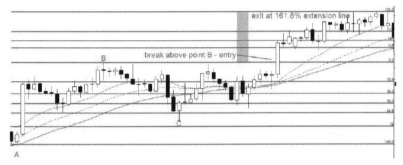

5.2. *Example of entry in the safe scenario.*

The disadvantage of this scenario is that sometimes the price will explode through a recent high/low and it will be hard to join the move. Do not worry – it happens sometimes. If you miss it, just wait for another correction. Sooner or later, there will be a strong correction, and maybe a better opportunity to enter the trade.

The key to success here is practice and patience. On some trading days you may have a couple of good or even very good setups and successful trades.

On other days you might end waiting for a setup the whole day and the market gives you nothing. It is important not to trade because you have to. Just wait and eventually a good trade setup will occur.

In the next example we can see a 4-hour silver chart. The main trend is up, so we want to buy silver. Finally, we identified the AB swing and waited for a correction which turned out very mild. Our entry point is when the price closes above point B, which, in this case, was very rapid. Take a close look at the chart and notice how fast the move was. In a few hours the price climbed up to the 161.8% extension line which was strong resistance and the best exit point. Right afterwards, there was a strong sell off. Those using the lagging indicators probably ended with a loss.

5.3. *Strong breakout and good opportunity to go long in safe scenario.*

Let's take a look at how this strategy can be used in a downtrend. On the chart below we have a WTI oil daily chart. The trend is down, so we look to take a short position (sell WTI). It is easy to find the AB swing. The correction ended at point C (78% retracement line). We wait for a breakdown below point B where we enter a short position. The move down was very strong and it ended at the 200% extension line.

Where to place the stop loss in the safe scenario?

In this scenario you place your stop loss not so far away from the entry point. You assume that a break above the last peak should lead to a strong move. If, after a while, the price fails to move forward and comes back to the retracement levels, there is probably something wrong with the trend strength (at least at that moment). You do not want to wait and see if 38.2% or 61.8% will hold as support because the price was there already and you have a position opened at the last peak! What you want to do in this case is closing the position as soon as something goes wrong.

My advice is: when the price moves back below the 23.6% retracement level, close your trade. Of course, do it with the stop loss order – do not wait and hope for the best.

5.5. *Placing stop loss in a safe scenario.*

The stop loss behind 23.6% is only my recommendation, but feel free to change it. Maybe you will want to have a tighter stop? Then try to set your stop loss order behind the 14.6% retracement line (it is also a retracement level, but I have hidden it on my chart).

Setting the stop much wider behind 23.6% is not a good idea in my opinion. We hunt for a strong move forwards to the extension line. If the price does not move in that direction, this trade should be closed by our stop loss order.

Which breakout is correct?

Sometimes you may get confused which breakout is correct. You have probably heard about false breakouts. In order to avoid this, just wait for the close of the candle and check the closing price. If you look at the 1-hour chart, each candle closes after 1 hour and there is another candle on the chart. When the close of the candle is on the other side of the resistance/support line, you have your correct breakout. In the example below we can look at a breakdown. The support line is at 1294 points. The first breakdown was false, but the close of that candle was above the support line. Later, there was another breakdown, but this time the close of the candle was below the support line. This was our signal to enter short.

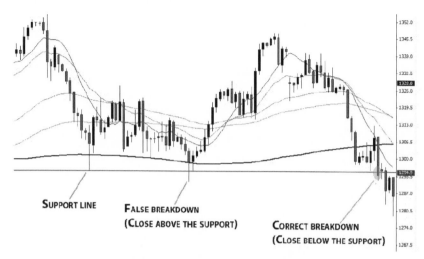

SUPPORT LINE   FALSE BREAKDOWN
(CLOSE ABOVE THE SUPPORT)

CORRECT BREAKDOWN
(CLOSE BELOW THE SUPPORT)

5.6.   *The confirmation signal in a safe scenario.*

Of course, this confirmation is not 100% accurate, but with this method you have a better chance of success. It will help you avoid many false breakouts.

The win/loss ratio

The overall win/loss ratio is very good with this method. I know of traders who have won around 70% of their trades with that method! It is a great result! Some traders have had even better results, some have had worse, but it is your main goal as it comes to the /loss ratio.

You do not have to achieve the 70% win ratio to be profitable. A ratio around 50% should give you a positive balance in your account. It is all possible thanks to tight stop losses. You risk little and you are likely to gain more. Some trades will be closed at the 127% extension line with small profit. But as you will see, some of them may last to the 161.8% extension or even longer! It is a good risk/reward proportion!

CHAPTER 6: TECHNIQUES FOR MAXIMIZING PROFITS

In this scenario you are going to take bigger risk, but in exchange for possible bigger profit.

Remember: this is a more risky way of trading with Fibonacci. Try to master the first method which is safer for new traders. Later, when you will feel more confident, try this method.

The game plan

With this method we want to enter a trade earlier, somewhere between points B and C, after a confirmation signal:

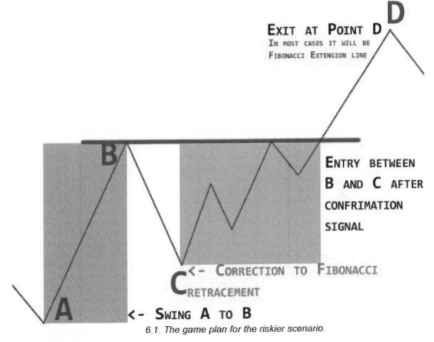

6.1. The game plan for the riskier scenario.

The first few points are the same as in the previous method, but they differ later on.

1. Identify the main trend. You should know what the main trend is and which direction you will be looking in to enter a trade.
2. Identify the low-high/high-low swing. Find the swing which you will draw the retracement and extension lines from.

3. Wait for the correction to part C to end. When there is a bounce back from the retracement line, get ready.
4. **Wait for a confirmation signal**. When there is a signal, enter the trade.
5. Close the trade at one of extension lines (later I will show you how).

So as not to confuse you, I will write more about confirmation signals in a separate part. Now, let's focus on the logic of this method.

You know what the trend direction is, so you know in which direction you will be opening the trade. After a low-high swing you wait for a correction to point C. You do not open a position right at the retracement line, because it is too risky. You simply wait for the price to accept the retracement line as support (or resistance). When the price goes back to move in a trend direction, there should be a signal somewhere between point C (retracement line) and point B.

What kind of signal? It depends on the trader. It may be a signal from the price action, oscillator, trend line or moving average. There are some good candidates here. You will read more about it shortly.

Let's take a look at the example. The signal was a break above the resistance line.

6.2. Entry after signal to go long – riskier scenario example.

You enter a trade between points B and C, that is, earlier than in the previous, safer scenario. Because of that, your possible profit is larger, but so is the risk.

Where to place the stop loss in this scenario?

Again, the stop loss should not be placed too wide. Remember, this is a risky scenario, so the possibility that the move will not continue in the trend direction is bigger.

There are a few scenarios here, when it comes to setting the stop losses.

C ends at 38.2%

The move is wide and the retracement levels are far away from each other. You decide to enter after the correction to the 38.2% line. My advice is to place the stop loss behind the next retracement line or the recent low. Remember, it was after you entered the trade with your signal.

6.3. Placing stop loss in riskier scenario.

On certain occasions, when I confirmed that the main trend on a higher time frame was very strong, I would place a wider stop loss (below 61.8% or 78%). The reason for that is that even if my signal was false, I still assumed that after a deeper correction, the price would go with main trend. However, when the AB swing is very long, then the retracement lines may be far away from each other (a bigger potential loss).

This is a tricky trade. There is always a chance that the price will go lower, to the 50% or 61.8% retracement. When you place the trade, you are not 100% sure that point C was at the 38.2% line.

If you still decide to open the position between 38.2% and point B, open a smaller position and add later, after the breakout.

C ends deeper

When the correction is deeper, up to 50% or 61.8%, I place my stops behind the 78% line or recent low.

6.4. Placing stop loss when correction is deep.

When C ends on the 78% retracement, I place my stop behind the 100% point (that is, below point A).

These are only propositions of where you can place your stop losses. You should test various scenarios and choose the one that works best for you. Always remember that the most important rule is to protect your capital.

The confirmation signals

When you decide which direction you want to open position in, you have to know when to do it. It is a good idea to define a set of entry and exit signals that you will follow. This way, you won't be making trading decisions based mostly on your emotions.

It is not enough to define a correct trend, draw the retracement levels and enter the position blindly between points A and B. You should have some signal to enter and exit. First, let's focus on the entry signals.

The close above/below the moving average

The signal I use often is closely above (or below in the down trend) the 50 moving average (50 MA). This is an important MA and, on many occasions, when the price closes above that line, it is a sign that the sentiment is changing. As on the chart below, after the correction to 78%, I would wait and enter after the candle closes back above the 50 MA (red line).

6.5. Confirmation signal – close above MA.

The moving averages crossover

Some traders like to wait for the moving averages crossover. Of course, this is a lagging signal, but that is what we want to have. We want confirmation that the correction might be over and it is a good moment to enter the position.

What periods of the moving averages are the best? It is up to you. Some prefer faster MAs (you get a signal earlier, but there is a higher risk that it might be false), whilst others like slower averages.

In the example below there are two simple moving averages: 10 SMA (red) and 20 SMA (blue). The main trend is down, after the correction up to 78%, the price falls back. When the red MA crosses with blue MA, we get our signal to enter a short position.

6.6. Cross of the averages as a confirmation signal.

Try to use the moving averages of other periods, 10 and 20 are the example here. Test other combinations, such as 5 and 15, 8 and 13, 8 and 21, 20 and 33, or if you want to use slower MAs, check 33 and 55.

Why not simply give you one set of MAs to follow? Because some traders trade on 4-hour EUR/USD and some MAs work better than others there. Other traders prefer EUR/USD, but on a 5-minutes chart, and here other MAs may be a better choice. Can you see how many combinations there can be? You have to learn how to choose the best MAs for individual stock, index or currency.

The trend lines

Sometimes you do not need to use tools like the moving averages. If you have some experience in drawing the trend lines, it is also a good way to look for where to enter the position.

In the example below, the price is in a down trend. When a correction occurs, we can draw the trend line.

The price moved to the 38.2% level and down below the green trend line. It turned out that this was a false signal. In the next move, after hitting the 50% level, there was a break below the red support line. This signal was correct and it was a good place to enter the position.

first break below trend line was false

second break was a good entry point

6.7. Break below support line as a signal to go short.

The Williams %R as confirmation

You can use oscillators as a source of a confirmation signal. If you have your favorite oscillator, test it and check what signals work as best confirmation.

My favorite one is the Williams %R. Most of the time, I use it for 33 back periods. For time frames lower than 1 hour, I use 55 periods.

It is a slightly different oscillator, because its range is between 0 (at the top) and -100 (at the bottom). When the line is between 0 and -20, then the price is overbought. When the line is between -100 and -80, the price is oversold; similarly to the stochastic oscillator, but the levels are different.

What I look for as regards the Williams %R are two things:

1. A break of important support/resistance on an oscillator – I use it especially when the price action is not clear for me.

Many people do not know that you can draw support, resistance and trend lines on the oscillators also! I find it to be very useful. When the price action is too blurry for me, I look for some tips on an oscillator chart by drawing the trend lines there.

2. A break in the overbought or oversold area.

In an uptrend, when there is a correction, I look at the oscillator and wait until its value is back at the -20 level and then I enter a long position.

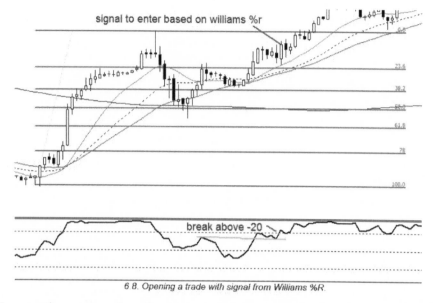

6 8. Opening a trade with signal from Williams %R.

In another example, there is a strong trend down. There is a correction, but the price action is not that clear. What I look for is the %R back at the -80 line. When it happens, I enter my short trade.

It is not a 100% correct signal and it is not the best tool to choose in all cases. In my trading, I find this to be quite good and effective. With good money management and using the Williams %R, your results should be better.

Examples

Below you can see a weekly chart of copper. After the correction to the 38.2% retracement line, the price closed back above the 50 moving average. This was the entry signal, and it turned out to be the right one.

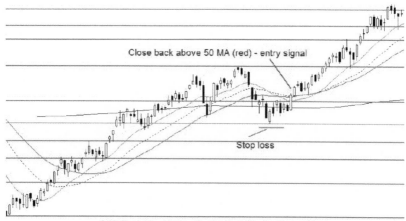

6.10. Example of entry after break above moving average.

I only use this method strong trends like the one above. When the trend is weaker, it is more possible that this signal may be a false one.

Let's go back to the example with the WTI oil from the part about the safe scenario. The black moving average is a 200 SMA. You can see that it had been working as support for a long period of time (the blue rectangle). After that, there was a correction to the 78% retracement line and then a move back below the 200 simple moving average. When the price closed below that line, it was a good place to enter the short position. Why? Something changed. Suddenly, the MA stopped working as support and the price moved below it. That was the sign for traders.

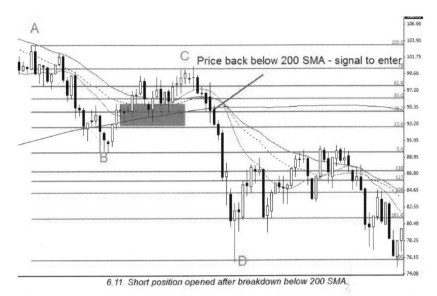

6.11. Short position opened after breakdown below 200 SMA.

In another example, a daily chart of oil is presented. It is easy to draw the resistance line. After the close above it, there was a good place to enter.

6.12. Long position opened after break above resistance line.

The range trading

It is not always so easy and obvious to trade with the Fibonacci tools. Not every move is a clear A to B, correction to C and then strong move up to point D at the extension. Sometimes, the correction to C may last longer. An attempt to break towards the extension may be a failure.

On the chart below you can see that the correction ended at the 38.2% retracement level, but the price failed to move up to the next high.

6.13. Range between Fibonacci levels.

You can see that, from that moment, the price moved in the range between the last high and the 38.2% line. Eventually, it broke up but, for a long period of time, it was not going in any particular direction.

This is something you can see on numerous occasions. The price range will very often be between the recent high/low and the Fibonacci retracement levels.

The move will not always continue in the main direction. A range means that there is no winning side there at the moment. Bulls and bears are struggling, eventually, one side wins. In the example below, the main trend is up, then there is a correction, but the bulls fail to move to the next high. For a while, there is a range move, but, in the end, the bears took control and the EUR/USD price started to fall.

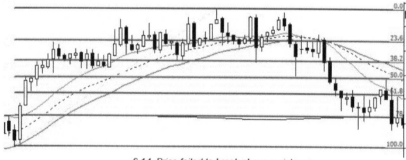

6.14. Price failed to break above resistance.

In the foregoing chart we could observe a narrow range. There are also wide ranges. A good example is a daily chart of EUR/USD. Here you can see that the 78% and 61.8% lines act as strong resistance in the range move.

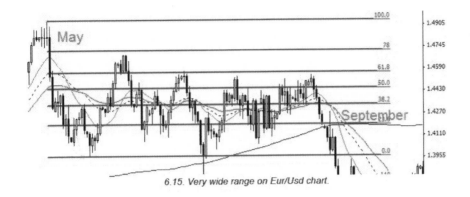

6.15. Very wide range on Eur/Usd chart.

Notice that this rage lasted since May till September! All that time there was no clear direction and investors were confused. That is why it is good to know that, on numerous occasions, the range is between the Fibonacci levels. The best thing about it is that you can trade it.

In order to do this, you can seek some help with oscillators, such as stochastic, RSI or ADX. The idea is simple here – you buy at support and sell at resistance. It sounds simple, but it is quite hard at the beginning. It is far different from the trend trading, but still, you can make money in a range. As you can see above –these skills are sometimes useful.

In this e-book, I focus on trading with Fibonacci in the trending markets. Trading in a range and using oscillators as entry/exit signals is a very wide topic.

My advice is to practice the range trading using a demo account. With your real account, go for trades you know how to trade and have succeeded with in your previous setups. When there is a range, do not trade your real money in it, trade using the demo account. With time, you will get better at this and you will have bigger experience. One day, when you feel strong enough, you will include this in your trading plan.

CHAPTER 7: IDEAL TIME TO EXIT A TRADE

In this chapter I will show you what the best methods of exiting positions are. With the Fibonacci extension tool, it is quite easy to get ahead of other investors.

Way no. 1

The tool we will be using to define the exit point is the Fibonacci extension. If you do not remember what it is, go back to Part 3 and read it once again.

There are some rules which traders follow, basing on how deep the correction was. Have a look at the table below and then move on to examples.

Correction to:	Look for the exit at the extension of:
38.2%	138.2%
50%	161.8%
61.8%	161.8%

The best way to explain this method is upon examples.

Let's assume that we have found an uptrend. We wait for a correction to enter a long position. Correction is shallow, **only the 38.2% retracement** line. We go long and now there is a question –**when to close this trade?** Many traders follow the rule that the move up from the 38.2% retracement may **end at the 138.2% extension** line (exactly as in the table presented).

It is not something written in the stone. They are simply aware of the statistics and probability. They know that there is a big chance that the move will end or stop for a while there.

Check the daily chart of EUR/USD. The small correction ended at 38.2% and after that, the price continued to move up. Eventually, there was resistance just at the 138.2% extension line.

7.1. Move to 138.2% extension line.

When the correction is deeper, there is a greater chance that the continuation of the main move will be stronger. As you can see in the table, a correction to a 50%, 61.8% or 78% retracement may lead to a stronger move up to the 161.8% extension level.

In next example, there is an hourly chart of S&P500 index presented. From a higher time frame we know that the main trend is down. There is a correction ending at the 61.8% extension. Pay attention that this is just below the 200 SMA – this is information for traders that the move may end there. After the correction, the S&P500 moves down and ends exactly at the 161.8% extension. So as it can be seen in the table – there is a move from 61.8% to 161.8%.

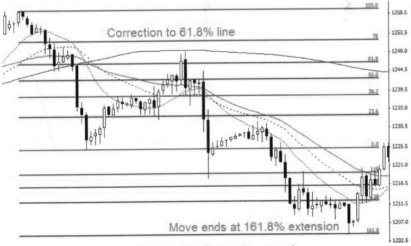

7.2. Move to 161.8% extension – example.

On the daily EUR/USD chart there was a correction down to the 50% retracement. Then, buyers came back, the 200 SMA (strong resistance before) was broken and euro started to move up strong. The move lasted up to the 161.8% extension.

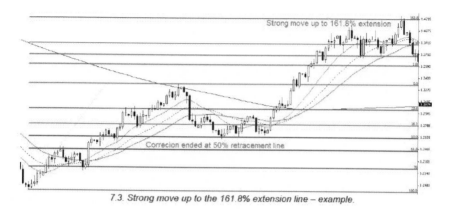

7.3. Strong move up to the 161.8% extension line – example.

Does it always work like this? Should you simply buy at 50% and sell at 161.8%? Is it that simple? No, it is not. It does not always work like this. In the example below, after a shallow correction to the 38.2% line, there is a strong move up to 161.8%.

7.4. Another example of move to the 161.8% extension line.

Has there been anything wrong with the table from the very beginning of the chapter? No, the table is just fine. You have to understand that it is about probability. As I mentioned before, there is a chance that the move from the 38.2% line would extend to **at least** 138.2%. It sometimes ends before that level, and sometimes the price moves further on.

How to use the table?

You have seen some examples of situations when the connections between the correction and extension move are very accurate. There are cases when they are not so useful. So, when to use the table? Whenever you are in doubt when to close your trade, it is wise to follow this rule. Remember, we are not here to catch bottoms and tops. We just want to make money. When you see that the price action is fast and you are confused about it, follow the table.

You can connect this with the money management system. Divide your position into 2 or 3 parts. Close the bigger part at the extension level based on the table, and let the rest of the position catch the rest of the move or scratch it when the move ends.

Let me assure you that, having a plan of when to exit, you place yourself in the top 20% of traders. The remaining 80% have no idea when to exit. They just go with the flow, hoping for the best. In the meantime, you make money.

Is it perfect? No, but it is a plan and you can include it into your trading plan.

Setting an exit place

When you are placing an exit order, it is a good idea to place it just before the level you plan to exit at. You should practice it yourself, but my advice is to place exit orders a few points earlier than the exit level. There are two reasons for that.

Sometimes, the price will not touch the extension line, like in the previous examples. It may miss it just by a few points and it will still be a valid move to the Fibonacci extension line.

Another reason is that when the price reaches a certain extension line, you are not the only one trying to exit. The price might just touch the line and move back fast and your close order may not be completed.

By setting an exit point just in front of the extension line you increase your chances to close your trade with profit.

Surely, on certain occasions the price will move beyond the extension line. That is the life of a trader. The most important thing is to have a plan which can give you good exit points, and not tops and bottoms.

I have one observation regarding this way of closing positions.

The lower time frame you trade, the more you should follow rules from the table. On lower time frames, moves are very fast. People and "robots" trade here very actively and you should adjust to it. Do not try to catch the whole move from the beginning to the end. There are many opportunities here. Are you in a profitable trade? It is great. Now, if you are not sure where to exit, follow the table.

Way no. 2

Exiting a trade is very important, yet it is not so easy. We want to exit at the very best moment, but it is hard to tell when this moment comes. What is worse, the price very often climbs slowly to a certain level, and then suddenly it can fall hard.

Trying to exit at the top does not make sense, because there is always a chance that there will be another top and this one is only a stop. Be not concerned about catching tops.

In order to define a good exit point, we have to connect the Fibonacci extension levels, technical analysis and money management. With this, it is easier to decide when to close the position. I am not going to cheat you – on numerous occasions you will close your trade too early or too late. It is normal and you have to work on your exit strategy to make it better.

Any exit plan is better than simply letting the trade run and hoping for the best.

Thanks to the Fibonacci extension we get the potential levels where the price will stop, or where even the whole trend can stop and reverse. As you have seen in the previous chapter, it can be very accurate. The problem is that we do not know which of those levels is going to work.

That is why we use money management. You can read more in the chapter about money management, and now I will show you a good way of using the MM in closing trades.

When it looks like that you have been correct and your trade is profitable, you move your stop loss to the entry point. This way, even when the price moves back, you will protect your capital.

The 3 parts rule

Next, you have to divide your position into three parts. You close the first part right at the 127% extension. If the price still goes according to the trend, you close the second part at the 161.8% extension (or at 138.2% if you think that the trend is not so strong). You let the third part to rise and you can close it manually at a different extension level or a technical trigger.

This way, you protect your profit, but you let it grow.

In the example below, the correction ends at the 61.8% retracement level. The entry signal is the close of the candle above the 50 moving average. When the trade is profitable, the 1st part is closed at the 127% extension. It continues to rise, so the 2nd part is closed at the 161.8% extension. The 3rd part is still open. You can close it manually at any moment.

7.5. Money management and closing trade in parts.

This trend is strong, but if you are in doubt, you should close the 2nd part at the 138% extension. More probably, trend will stop for longer a time and we just want to protect profits!

Sometimes, only the first target will be hit and the price won't reach the next Fibonacci level.

In the example below, a down trend can be identified. The correction is deep, up to the 78% retracement level, the entry point is after the close below the 50 MA.

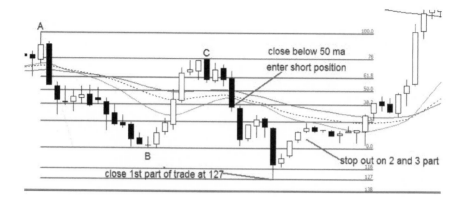

7.6. Move down to the 127% extension and strong bounce back.

It is going nicely down to the 127% extension, where the 1st part of the position gets closed. Suddenly, buyers show up and start to buy. The price reverses and starts to rise. There are still 2 parts of the position open, but the stop loss is raised to the entry point. It is important to remember to raise your stop loss to the entry point while managing your trade.

The rise continues and eventually we get stopped out, but still, we close the trade with a profit. All thanks to the 1st part closed at the 127% extension and the raised stop loss.

This is how it works. At times, you get lucky, the trend is strong and you close all three parts at higher levels. On other occasion you will be stopped out with a loss, or only a small profit from the first extension level.

If this rule is a too complicated for you, start from dividing your position into two parts. When you manage your trades carefully, you should be making good money on it.

This is the main way I manage my trades, but you may want to choose some technical tool to confirm the exit signal (for example for parts 2 and 3). In such a case I would recommend something simple. Just lower your time frame. If you trade with a 4-hour chart, lower it to a 1-hour chart and watch the reaction of the price and the extension levels closely. You can draw some short moving average (5 or 10 periods) as help.

CHAPTER 8: EXCELLENT TEMPLATES FOR OPTIMIZING TRADE RESULTS

At the beginning, it might be hard for you to decide in which direction you should trade or even take a position at the moment. That is why I have prepared this template for Meta-trader, which will help you make better decisions.

What can you see on the chart? Let's go through this:

- A candlestick chart

- The 200 simple moving average

- The linear weighted moving averages from 5 to 154 periods long (the rainbow)

- Two Kijun-sen lines from Ichimoku (one is 26 periods long and and the other is 60 periods long)

It may look like there are a lot of things on the chart, but this is only to help you visualize what the current situation is. Go to the end of the e-book to read how to install this template in detail.

Candlesticks and the 200 simple moving average should be familiar to you by now. Let's discuss the other tools in detail.

The linear weighted moving averages from 5 to 154 periods are also called the rainbow. There are many types of the rainbow chart – sometimes they are built from averages ranging from 2 to 200 periods. In this case, we have averages from 5 to 154 sorted in three groups: blue, green and red. You look at them to find out what the current trend is and how strong it is. It is very simple. When the blue group is at the bottom, green in the middle and red at the top, then we probably have a strong downtrend.

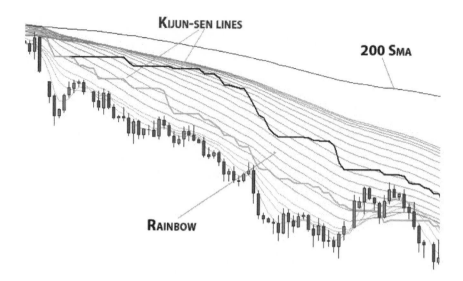

When there is an opposite situation – blue at the top, green in the middle and red at the bottom there is probably a strong uptrend.

When these averages are mixed up, there is probably something wrong with the trend.

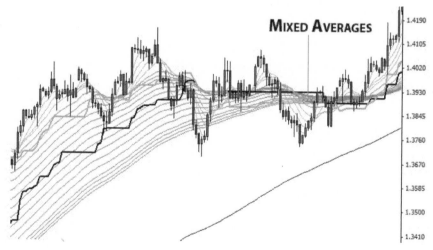

We use the rainbow to have another confirmation of the current trend. Of course, we could achieve a similar goal with a set of a few averages, but I like the look of the rainbow. It is very intuitive to use.

The Kijun-Sen lines

These are lines taken from the Ichimoku Kinko Hyo indicator. Actually, in Ichimoku there is only one Kijun-sen line, and a few other lines, but I've taken two Kijun-sen lines with different parameters. What is so great about these lines? The price respects them and if there is an uptrend, the price for sticks above them most of the time. If there is a downtrend, the price is below these lines most of the time.

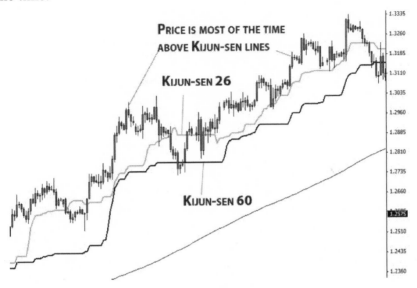

How to use this template?

Basically you should search for a situation to take the long position when:

- The price is above 200 SMA
- The rainbow lines suggest an uptrend
- The shorter Kijun-sen is above the longer Kijun-sen

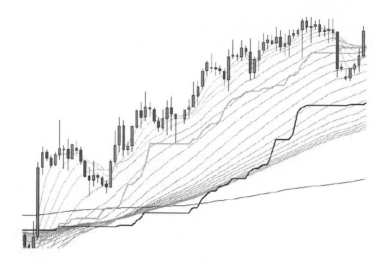

In order to take the short position, you look for a situation when:

- The price is below 200 SMA
- The rainbow lines suggest a downtrend
- The shorter Kijun-sen is below the longer Kijun-sen

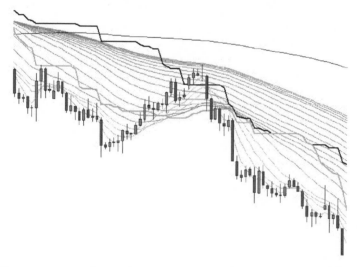

Now you can draw the retracement lines and place the trade in the direction of the trend. Of course, it is not always perfect, but in the situation described above you have the best chance of success. Let's have a look at two examples.

Below we can see a very strong uptrend on a 4-hour chart of EUR/USD. It is a perfect situation to use the Fibonacci retracement and extension tools. The trend is strong, so it is very easy to find many ABCD setups. Below you can see one of them. Notice that you could draw more of those on that chart.

Now let's see what it looks like in the downtrend. Notice that the moving averages suggest a downtrend. There is also a confirmation from the Kijun-Sen lines. We know that the safest option here is to look for an ABCD pattern for a short opportunity. After a strong correction, there is one great opportunity.

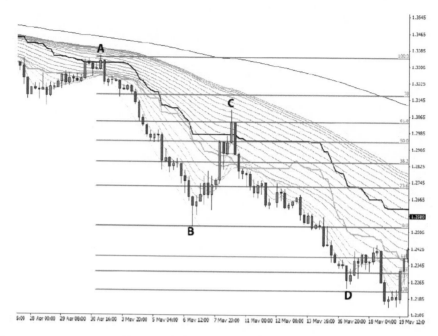

You can spot the logic here. This template is only helps me to make sure that I am investing in the right direction. I find it very useful and I hope you can make use of it too.

CHAPTER 9: CRUCIAL ELEMENTS IN DETERMINING MARKET TREND AND MOVEMENT

In this part I will focus on a few different things you should know and be aware of in the trading journey.

How to define a trend?

The key to successful trading with Fibonacci is to trade in the direction of the main trend. That is why you draw the retracement levels. You want to enter the trade with a better price. You do not want to buy blindly at some random place and guess the direction of the trend. You define the trend, wait for the correction and take a position in the same direction as the trend goes.

If the trend is up, you go long (that is, you buy).

If the trend is down, you go short (that is, you sell).

When there is no trend in place, you do not take any position.

It sounds simple, but it is not that easy to define the correct direction of the trend. Unfortunately, it is necessary to open a position in the right direction to make money. If the trend is up and you go short, you will most likely end with a loss.

What is worse, if you make a mistake and define the trend incorrectly, you might be fooled by Fibonacci, because it works in both ways. Let me show you what I mean. Below you can see the retracement levels and a bounce from 61.8%. Basing on this chart you might think that going long is a good idea.

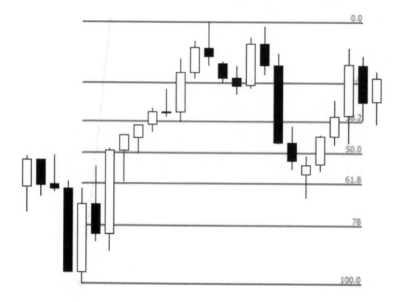

Unfortunately, going long is a wrong decision, because the main trend is down, which you can see on the bigger chart:

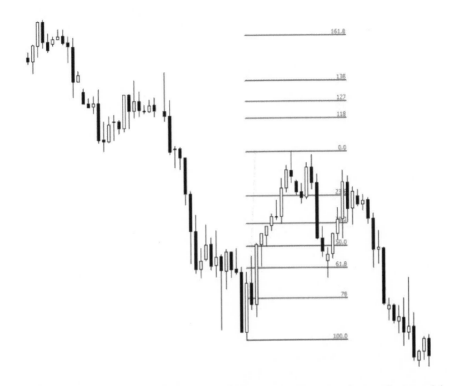

Notice that there is a price bounce from 61.8%, but the main trend is down! You should look for other Fibonacci retracement lines, so that you can enter a short position (not long).

You will not be 100% correct every time when it comes to deciding in which direction you should draw the retracement levels and place a trade order. You should have some tools which will help you to recognize in which direction the main trend goes.

There are many tools to choose among, but I will give you some propositions. Test them and choose the one which works best for you.

Look at the chart from a distance

This is a well-known piece of advice and it works. Leave the price only on chart and zoom out. What is the direction of the trend? You should be able to spot it easily. If not, there might not be a strong trend at the moment.

If you are confused, some say you should look at the chart with the eyes of a child. It is not as silly as it might sound like. Children do not overanalyze things. If something is black, it is black. If the price goes up, then it goes up. Children do not look for some hidden message which other might not know about. Next time, just look at the chart from a distance and try to define the trend at first sight.

On the chart below, the main trend is definitely up:

Identify highs and lows

When the trend is up, the price makes higher highs and higher lows.

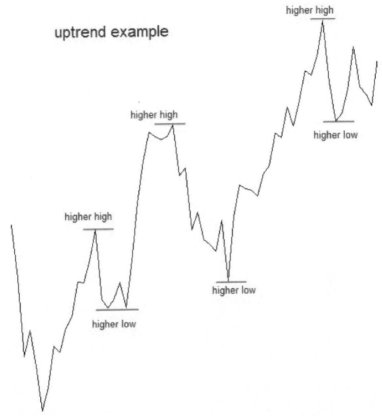

uptrend example

higher high

higher high

higher high

higher high

higher low

higher low

higher low

When the trend is down, the price makes lower highs and lower lows.

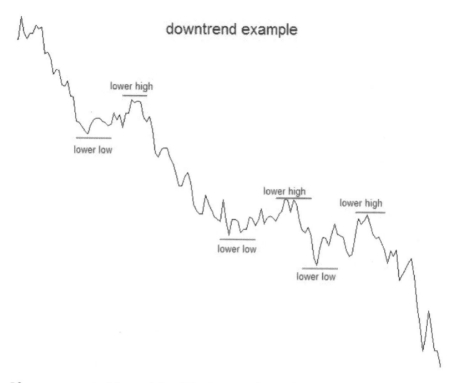

downtrend example

lower high

lower low

lower high

lower low

lower high

lower low

If you are not able to identify these points, there is a chance that the price is not moving in one direction.

This is a simple technique and you just need to practice it. You can start with using a line chart only, as it is easier to read, but in the end you should use a candlestick chart.

Use the technical analysis tools

You can use the technical analysis tools as help in identifying the current trend. It might be something as simple as the 200 simple moving average. When the price is above that line, you only look for long positions. When the price is below, you only go short.

It is a very simple and yet, an effective tool. Of course, you may want to use a shorter moving average like the 100 SMA. Some traders use an even shorter MA, such as a 50 or 30 periods long. It is up to you.

On the chart below, the price is above the 200 SMA, so you draw the retracement levels only to look for long opportunities.

My set of tools

I personally use three moving averages:

- The 20 linear weighted moving average (typical price)
- The 35 linear weighted moving average (typical price)
- The 50 linear weighted moving average (typical price)

If the 20 MA is above the 35 MA and the 50 MA, and the 35 MA is in the middle, then the main trend is probably up and I open a long position.

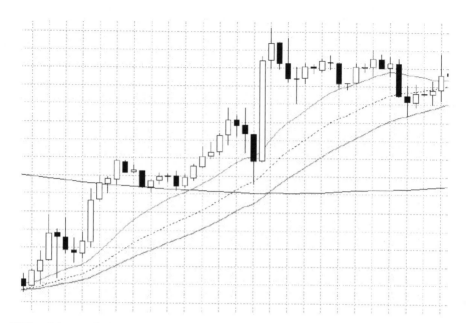

If the 20 MA is below the 35 MA and the 50 MA, and the 35 MA is in middle, then the main trend is probably down and I only open a short position.

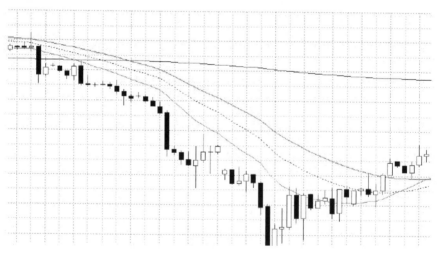

If I am not sure what the current trend is (for example, when the moving averages are mixed up), I hold and do not trade.

The importance of the higher time frame

Now you have the tools to enter the position and you know how to manage your position to exit at a good moment. If there is a trend in place and you have correctly identified the direction of the trend, you are halfway to a successful trade.

Next, you have to choose the correct swing to draw the retracement lines, enter the position at the correction and exit at the extension. It sounds simple and it is just that – if you are investing in a the right direction.

It may be a huge problem, because sometimes the trend is not so clear to see. The trend may be there, but the price action may seem very mixed up to you. Which direction is it anyway? And which swing should you choose? How to avoid confusion?

As a smart person, you probably know the answer, basing on the title of this part. The higher time frame is vital help.

You have to learn how to use it every time when you are in doubt. Testing the higher time frame is a good idea, because it gives you the answers to your questions.

It looks like an uptrend, but is it one? On the 4-hour chart you can see that, in fact, the trend is up after some correction:

That way you get a clearer picture of the current situation.

Remember: if you are not sure about the direction of the trend, check the higher time frame.

There is one more important thing I would like you to remember and use. It increases your chance of success substantially.

The rule is simple:

<u>**Always trade in the direction of the trend from the higher time frame.**</u>

An example may be very helpful here to convince you to use the rule. Below you can see a 15-min chart of EUR/USD.

Clearly, there is a trend change and you can spot the correction. When you draw the retracement levels, it looks as if it was working. So, is it a good place to go short?

In order to make sure, we check the higher time frame. Below you can see the same pair, but on a 1-hour chart.

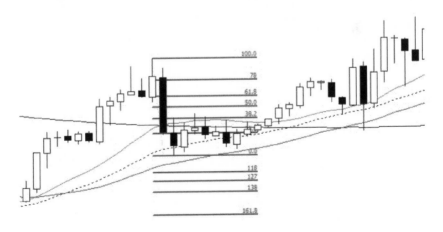

Wait a minute! Going short was a bad idea, because the main trend is up. That was only a correction. Notice that the retracement levels seemed to fit perfectly. It looked like the 38.2% retracement level was going to stop the price. As I have mentioned earlier, you have to be very careful because the Fibonacci retracement levels work both ways and it is your job to identify the correct trend. In the example it looked like you should the draw retracement levels for a short position, but the higher time frame gave you an answer not to.

In another example, we look to take a long position at the S&P500 index. On a 1-hour chart it looks like an uptrend, and there is a potential swing where we can draw the retracement levels:

In order to make sure, we check with the higher time frame, in this case, on a 4-hour chart. When you look at left side, there is a clear uptrend.

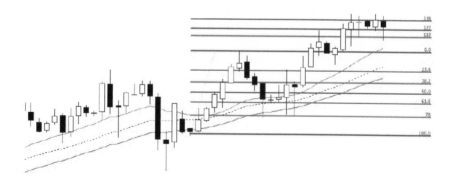

The correction ended and new highs were made, which stopped at the 138% extension from that move.

The logic behind this is obvious. The trend from the higher time frame is going to last longer, so it is stronger. When there is a correction, on the lower time frame it looks like there is a change of the trend direction. However, it is not the truth. The correction ends on the higher time frame and the price moves in the previous direction.

Remember about that simple rule and always invest in the direction of the higher time frame. This way, your win/loss ratio will be much higher.

Trading the news with Fibonacci

If you want to trade in the Forex market, you should be aware of the news schedule. Every day there is a lot of economic news from many countries. Most of it is not so important, but there is some news that the market waits for and reacts strongly to their announcement.

If you trade Forex, you should know what economic data will be published. You can check this, for example, on forexfactory.com. In a table on the site there is a column named impact, which represents the impact of the news on the market.

Some of the most important news is the rate decisions and the non-farm payrolls (NFP). The US non-farm payrolls are published at 1.30 p.m. (London time) on the first Friday of each month.

The US non-farm payrolls release is one of the most closely watched US indicators, and is considered one of the best gauges of the US job creation.

The labour market is critically important for the US economy, with unemployment levels playing the leading role in the perceived strength of the current economic recovery. Consequently, the policies of the Federal Reserve may be influenced by the non-farm figures.

Nowadays, all markets are volatile and it is a good idea to trade less or even not to trade at all.

But there is a way you can still trade with good results. The Fibonacci tools are very useful here.

Before I show you how can you trade the news, there will be an important warning.

When you try to enter a position at the time the news is published, there might be a slippage. It means that the difference between the "ask" and the "bid" price may be considerable and the cost of entering the position may be very high. Check with your broker what their policy about slippage is.

Only risk a very small part of your capital for trading the news.

A lot of things can go wrong here, so do not risk too much!

You know the risk now, so let's see how to trade the news in practice. I will show you a chart from the time when the NFP were released. You can trade on the major pairs or main US indexes. In the examples below, I am going to use the SP500 chart.

The main idea is that the NFP release very often (but not always!) leads to a stronger move. This move is very specific. The first moment after the news release, short term traders are opening and closing positions - that is why there are a lot of messy moves. We do not want to trade the market like this, so we wait. After the news release, the data is known. Many investors holding back before the release, get back to trading. That is why the market starts to trend stronger. Where there is a trend, there are also corrections, and we can use the Fibonacci tools to enter and exit positions.

Look at the 1-minute chart from December 2nd. After the release, there was quite a mess for 5 minutes, but after that time a strong trend occurred.

You can probably see the retracement and extension clearly now. Yes, it is perfect to play with Fibonacci.

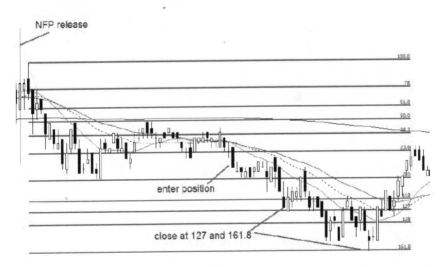

My advice is to exit at the extension level. Do not wait too long. When I trade on the news day, I usually divide my position into two parts. I close the first part at the 127% extension line, and the second at the 138.2% or 161.8% extension (depends on the price action).

What is interesting, later that day there was a number of strong moves. It was probably because after data was revealed, investors were taking positions again. You can find a lot of good situations to enter the short term position. For example, later the same day there was another good trade chance. When would you enter and exit?

This was a good day to practice your trading skills. There were a lot of opportunities where you could use the Fibonacci retracement and extension lines, but you had to make decisions quickly – in which direction should you open the trade? This is a very good opportunity to practice, but – again –risk was greater here! Remember about smaller positions!

Other Fibonacci tools

There are a number of Fibonacci tools you can use. Why is there so much information in this e-book about the Fibonacci retracement and extension lines and so little about other tools? It is because I base my trading plan on these tools and they are enough to trade successfully. So should you use other tools? Yes, but there are some things you should be aware of.

Using them all at once may be very confusing and you may end losing money because of information overload. When you draw your retracement, extension, time zones and fan on one chart, you see such a big area of support and resistance that it is simply too much. Do not do that.

It is very important to learn how to use tools like the retracement and extension first in order to be comfortable with them. Then, you can move on and use other tools, such as fan or arcs. You will understand how they work very quickly because the logic is similar to that of the extensions and retracements. You can find the 38.2%, 61.8% and other Fibonacci levels working as support/resistance, so it won't be something totally new for you.

CHAPTER 10: A GREAT COMBINATION BETWEEN FIBONACCI AND PIVOT POINTS

In this part you will learn how you can improve your results by using the Fibonacci technique and Pivot points together.

At the end of this e-book you will find a short instruction about how to install and use Pivot points.

What are Pivot points?

I want to show you how you can be more profitable by combining two leading indicators: Fibonacci and Pivot points. Firstly, a short introduction to Pivot points. The topic is wide and you only need some basic understanding of Pivot points, because the main trading tool will still be Fibonacci.

Pivot points are a set of horizontal lines calculated on the previous bars. There is a whole mathematical formula behind it, but as a result, you get the Pivot point line, which is always in the middle.

Above the Pivot line, there are also the resistance lines called R1, R2, R3 (you can count more, but the price rarely moves up to R3).

Below the Pivot line, you can find support lines called S1, S2, S3.

Below, you can see a 4-hour chart of EUR/JPY with the daily Pivot points:

The logic behind this tool is that the price will rise, but eventually, at some point, it will be oversold and it will be very hard for the buyers to force the resistance line. The R1, R2, R3 lines are calculated on the basis of the previous bars and help you determine where the resistance and overbought area might be. When the price is overbought, there is a strong chance that a correction may occur. Then it may take the price down to the Pivot line –that is, to the middle. If the move is strong, it may take the price even lower to the support levels S1 or S2.

On numerous occasions, this tool may be very accurate, so it is good to have it on the chart from time to time.

The most important levels to watch are the S2 and R2. At S2 many sellers close trades and buyers try to buy there. There is a chance for a strong bounce from the S2 level.

At R2 many traders close transactions and open short positions. A strong sell-off is possible at that level.

A monthly, weekly or daily Pivot?

There is one more important thing you should know. There are different Pivot point types. We can draw monthly Pivot points, weekly Pivot points, daily Pivot points and even 4-hour or more frequent ones. It is all because they are counted on the previous bar, so you may have the previous bar of the month with its high, low, close and count Pivot points for this month.

So as not to confuse you, I will suggest which Pivot points you should use. It all depends on the time frames you trade most.

Case 1:

You mainly trade on **very low time frames**: 1-min, 5-min...30-min...1-hour – you should have daily Pivot points on your chart. Weekly points are optional – if you want, you can have them too, but it is not necessary.

Case 2:

You trade on **medium time frames**: 4-hour or daily ones – you should be aware where the weekly and monthly Pivot points are. You should check the daily Pivot points only when you are opening a trade (not to open it at the daily R2 line).

Case 3:

You are a **long-term trader**. You trade on high time frames: daily, weekly or monthly ones. You should mostly have the monthly Pivot points, or even the quarterly ones.

Should you have all these drawn on your chart? No, unless you want to. It is very hard to read a chart when you have so many indicators on it.

When I trade with Fibonacci, I start a day with identifying the kind of trend there is, and then I check where the major resistance and support levels from Pivot points. Sometimes, I make a note and sometimes I just open another chart with the same index, stock or whatever I am trading at the moment. On the first chart I have the levels from Pivot points and on the second one I only have a few moving averages. When it comes to trading, I can quickly check if this is a good point to enter or exit a trade.

How to use Fibonacci and Pivots together?

Fibonacci and Pivot levels may give you an idea of where the strongest support or resistance may be. This way, you know better when to open and close the trade. I usually look for a convergence of the Fibonacci retracement line and the Pivot support line (S1, S2, S3) when I want to open a long position in an uptrend.

Let's have another look at the example where I showed you the Pivot points on the EUR/JPY chart. We can draw the Fibonacci retracement lines. Notice that when we do it, there is a clear convergence of the daily S2 level and the 50% Fibonacci retracement line. If you are looking to enter a long position, it is a great point to do that.

In another example, there is a trend up, and during a correction I go long. Over time my trade gets profitable, but I have to decide when I should close it. I trade on a 1-hour chart with weekly and monthly Pivot points. I look for the nearest resistance and I see that the nearest one is the weekly R1 line.

As stated before the most important are S2 and R2, but at R1 and S1 you can also expect some reaction, even if only a few hours long. Since I am opening the position for a short period of time, I do now need to check if there will be some reaction.

What is more, my extension level 118% is almost exactly in the same place as the weekly R1. Here we have a convergence of the Fibonacci extension line and the Pivot point resistance line. This is a red light for me. Now I know that I should not wait to see if the price goes up to the 138% or even 161.8% extension. I want to protect my profit. Of course the R1 level is not a brick wall and the price may go through it. In some cases it will move back and there will be a correction. I do not wait and I close the position at the 118% extension. Later the price moved a little bit higher, but as you can see, it went back, as a result.

I have my profit and I can hunt for another trade. I hope that you can now see why it is a good combination of tools. I still make my entry and exit decisions basing on Fibonacci, but Pivot points help me to decide when this entry and exit should take place. When I see a convergence of Fibonacci and Pivot lines, it is a very important sign for me that this level may be a strong resistance or support. Compare this technique with some trend following systems – how slow and lagging are they in comparison?

It is like information you heard on the radio that the road you are on is blocked or very icy. You can decide if you want to go back, select other route or just keep driving but try to be very careful.

Another, similar example: this time the price went higher above the weekly R1 resistance. Let's say you take a long position here and you are now in profit. When should you close the position?

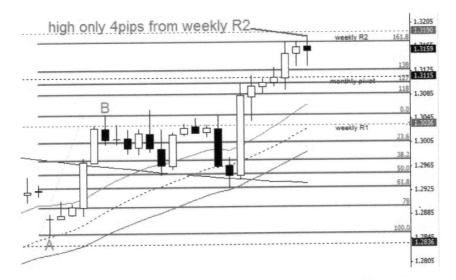

As you know after reading the previous parts of book, I suggest dividing the position into two or three parts. The first target here would be the 127% extension, because in the same area you can see the monthly Pivot. The price continues to rise and there is still part of the position open (let's say, another half in this case). You decide that the price is moving strong and there is a weekly R2 level ahead. You notice that just below the weekly R2 there is a 161.8% extension from the previous AB swing. Which level should you close at? In this case, the weekly R2 and 161.8% are very close to each other, so it is a good idea to close the position at this point.

Another way is to open the same chart and check the lower time frame. Sometimes the price tends to overshoot some resistance and then go back below. When you see the first signal of the price moving back, you close the second half of the position. In the example above, the price almost touched the weekly R2 (missed it only for 4 pips), but the 161.8% extension was holding the price.

From the beginning this trade was intended as a short term trade. Do you wait with opening the position and hope that the price will move up even more? As you remember the R2 leves tends to be a strong resistance. In the example above, it was Thursday when the price reached the weekly R2. Of course, there is a chance that on Friday there will be a continuation of the move up. But what if there is a correction and you still wait with your position open? You are going to lose most of your profit because the corrections are often very strong and fast.

When you follow my advice and you close your position in parts, you protect your profit. If you believe that there is a chance for the move to continue up, just leave 1/3 of your position open and watch how it goes.

Keeping the whole position open under the weekly R2 and 161.8% at the end of the week is not a good decision – you have to trust me on this one.

At the end of this e-book you can find instructions how to install Pivot points in the MetaTrader software. If this is too much information for you on one chart, just open another chart with the same index, stock or currency. Look how Fibonacci and Pivot point lines work great together sometimes. When you spot the convergence, you are much ahead of other traders!

CHAPTER 11: THE ROLE OF MONEY MANAGEMENT IN TRADING

Without good money management you cannot be successful in trading. Your money management plan does not have to be very complicated, but you should follow some basic rules.

Money management is very important. In my opinion, it is as important as the technical part of trading (in our case, trading with Fibonacci). You may be a great Fibonacci trader, but without good money management, you are still going to fail.

What does good money management mean? It means that you do not risk too much of your money and even after a lost trade you have capital to invest and build your wealth.

It is not enough to decide that you are not going to take risky trades. You are not able to switch off emotions completely. And where there are emotions, there are also mistakes. That is why you need a good plan. The best way is to write it down and correct when necessary. This plan should contain several positions:

- Your trading account size
- Maximum risk
- Where you place stops
- When you take profit
- Number of lost trades you stop trading after

Stop losses and the 1% rule

Some traders prefer not to set stop losses, because they are afraid of "stop loss hunting". I will not tell you what you should do, but unless you are a very experienced trader, forget about that and always set stop losses. It does more good than bad and it can protect you from a bigger loss. Let's assume that you haven't set the stop loss. Suddenly, the price falls down instead of rising as you wished. And it falls hard. You want to close the order, you know that it is something you should do, but some voice tells you to wait. You try to convince yourself that this is only a correction and it will end soon. Yeah, sure...

With a stop loss in place you curb your emotion levels to the minimum, so you do not have such doubts.

The other important thing is how much you should risk. You have probably heard about the 1% rule. Yes, 1% is not much, but it is a good rule. The main idea is that you shouldn't risk losing more than 1% of your whole trading capital. So, if your trading account is 10000$, you shouldn't risk more than 100$. I know what you are thinking right now: "with this rule I will have to place very small positions".

Yes, if you want to place bigger positions, increase your account size. I know this is hard, but you cannot count that you will get lucky and make 100.000$ out of 1000$.

Without a proper account size you are not able to create a good money management system, and therefore, most probably you are going fail soon. This is the harsh truth.

It is true especially in our case when we use the Fibonacci tools. Entries are fast, stop losses are tight, and our main goal is to get a few points of profit on the bigger leverage. To be able to do that, you must have enough money to invest.

If you are short of money but want to make millions, you start to take very risky positions and, as a result, you are probably going to lose everything.

What to do if your account is not big enough?

Do not worry if you do not have enough cash right now. Simply trade on the lower leverage. Thanks to this you will be able to keep the 1% risk ratio. Do not think that you are not going to make any good money with such small positions. Okay, you are probably not going to. But what you are going to gain is valuable experience and knowledge. It takes a lot of time to learn how to trade successfully. Use this time to figure out how to get more money that you can later invest.

This way, when you get enough money, you will be ready.

This is the right path to succeeding in investing. A very small percentage of traders have got rich starting from small amounts, such as 2000$.

Just stick to the 1% rule and you will be in the 10% of best traders who follow their money management.

What if I still do not like the 1% rule?

Look, I get it. It is not something easy to use, but this is a great tool to protect your capital, mostly from your grid. If you still want to risk more than 1%, and you believe that you are ready for it, I will give you some advice. Divide your trading capital and pay it into two separate accounts. It is best to keep a 80:20 proportion.

Now you have two accounts –in the first one there is 80% of your money, and the rest 20% is in the second one. You are going to trade both these accounts, but with a different approach. With the bigger one, you are still going to stick to the 1% rule. It is because this is where most of your money is and you want to protect it.

You are going to trade with a bigger risk using your second account, so you can increase the maximum loss you can take up to 3-4% of your account. It may not seem a lot, but believe me – it is. If you can make good investing decisions, both your accounts will grow, even the smaller one. You are going to have bigger profits from that account because your positions are going to be quite big.

If you fail to trade successfully, your loss won't be so painful. Of course, you are probably going to lose most money from your smaller account, but most of your cash is safer at in the bigger one.

As I have already said, I recommend using the 1% rule for all of your trading money. But if you want to trade bigger positions, try my way and divide your account into two separate ones. This way, you are going to monitor your readiness to trade big positions. If not, you should stick to the 1% rule and build your main account.

Raising the stop loss order

I have discussed this before, but let me explain it more deeply. You should remember to raise your stop loss order when your trade is profitable. You do not have to rise it to entry point immediately, but you can do this step by step.

You can plan it in advance. For example, my plan looks more or less like this.

I open a position and set the stop loss (for instance) 10 points below the entry point. The price is rising and is about to break through the recent high (point B). I raise my stop loss and it is now only 5 points below my entry point. The price continues to rise and my first target (the 127 extension) is hit. I close 1/3 of my position and raise the stop loss up to the entry point. At the moment I have a profitable trade. I have booked profit and even if things get worse and the price falls, my stop loss is at the entry point, so this will only scratch my position.

It is hard to learn to strictly follow the plan, but you should try anyhow. If necessary, write it down, print and hang over your desk.

Following the 1% rule and managing your trade by closing parts at the extensions and raising the stop loss increase your chances of success in trading considerably!

When you enter a trade, you place your stop loss in the first place, somewhere below the entry point (in the uptrend). When you see that your entry has been correct and the trend is going up nicely, you should raise your stop loss up to the entry point. This way, even when there is a strong sell-off, you just scratch your position and avoid loss.

In the example below, there is a 1-hour EUR/JPY chart. After a break above the resistance the 200 SMA, there is a great place to open the position. You place the stop loss below the moving averages, around 97.50 points.

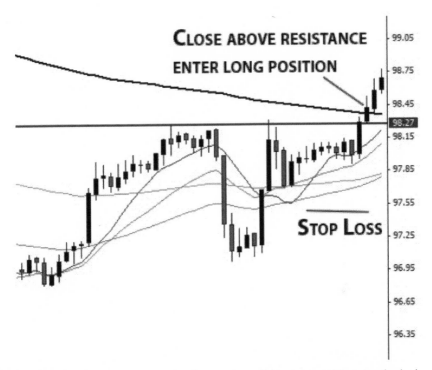

After several hours we can see that uptrend is strong. Our trade is in profit right now, so we can move our stop loss up to the entry point (around 98.40). This way, we can be sure that we won't lose in that trade.

If the trend continues upwards, we can raise the stop loss even more to make sure that we close the trade with profit.

It is a simple rule, but on numerous occasions it can help you save a lot of money.

CHAPTER 12: TYPICAL EXAMPLES OF TRADES USING FIBONACCI

Example 1. EUR/JPY trade

On the EUR/JPY daily chart you can see that there was a correction up to the 50% retracement line. Earlier, the 200 simple moving average worked as support, so it was best to wait until a price breakdown through the support. It took place at the end of April:

The breakdown here was the entry signal to take a short position at EUR/JPY. Earlier we have identified the ABC pattern, now we are looking for point D. The move down is very strong. There is some reaction at the 127% extension line – you could close some part of your position here. In this case I waited until the price reached the 161.8% extension – this was my point D and I closed my position there.

Later, there was an opportunity to reenter the short position when the price continued to move down.

Example 2. EUR/JPY on lower time frames

When you spot a situation like the one showed in the first example, remember that there may also be also a number of occasions to place good trade orders on lower time frames. When there is a break through an important support/resistance, lower your time frame and look for trade opportunities in the direction of the breakout. In the example there were plenty of trade opportunities on the 1-hour chart (and other time frames):

In the example above, there are two good entry signals. The first one after the break below the red trend line, the second one after the break below the support and the 0% Fibonacci line. The price went down to the 138% extension line and it was a good point to take profit. Look at the chart closely – later there was another breakdown and you could use the Fibonacci tools again to enter and exit another short position.

Example 3. Short at NZD/USD

In this example we can see a standard ABC pattern at the beginning of the downtrend. The correction went up to the 50% retracement line (our point C). After that there was a quick move down to the 127% extension line, which was the best place to take the profit or at least to close part of the position.

There are a few points you could enter the trade at, but let's focus on the bigger picture. After the move to point D there was another correction. You could draw other retracement lines for this move, but pay attention to how the extension lines from the first move were working. After another breakdown, there was a strong sell-off down to the 261.8% extension line from the first move.

This is a good example that you should, from time to time, also look at the extension lines from earlier moves.

Example 4. A failed breakout

In the example below you can see an AUD/USD 1-hour chart. There was a break above the 200 simple moving average and you could spot an ABC pattern. A few hours later there was a breakout with the close above the recent high. It looked like a good entry point and you would probably open a position here. Suddenly, there was a move back and a strong sell-off. That is why you should always have a stop loss order!

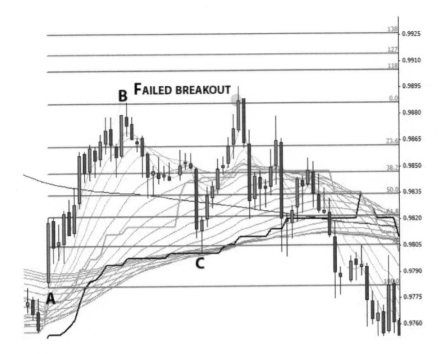

CHAPTER 13: HOW TO SET UP FIBONACCI IN META-TRADER PLATFORM

How to setup the retracement and extension lines together in Meta-Trader?

Select the Fibonacci retracement tool from the fast menu:

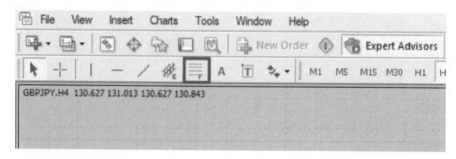

If you can't find it, go to the upper menu (**Insert**), click **Fibonacci** and select **Retracement**.

Draw the retracement lines on the chart:

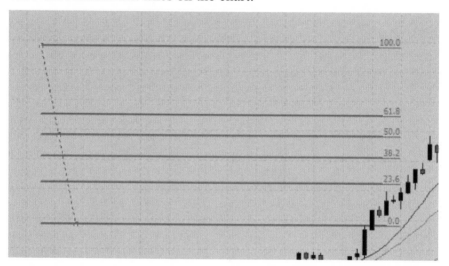

Select them so that the line going from 0 to 100 is highlighted. Now click the right mouse button and select the first option – **Fibo properties**.

In a new window, go to the second tab – **Fibo levels**. This is the place where you can add, remove or edit your Fibonacci levels. To edit value, just double click on it.

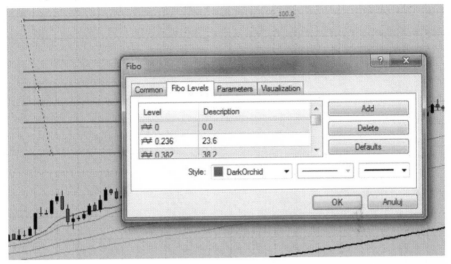

The first column in the table (**Level**) is a place where you define the level. The second column (**Description**) contains the description visible on the chart.

Now edit values in order to have levels as in the following table (the list is in the Level – Description order):

Level	Description
0	0
0.236	23.6
0.382	38.2
0.5	50.0
0.618	61.8
0.78	78
1	100
-0.18	118
-0.27	127
-0.382	138.2
-0.618	161.8

-1	200
1.618	261.8

As a result, you should have the retracement and extension lines as one tool:

	200
	161.8
	138
	127
	118
	0.0
	23.6
	38.2
	50.0
	61.8
	78
	100.0

In the future, you can edit these levels if you want to, but this set is more than enough for new traders.

How to draw them correctly?

It is simple. In a downtrend, when you look for a short opportunity, you draw the retracement **from high (A) to low (B):**

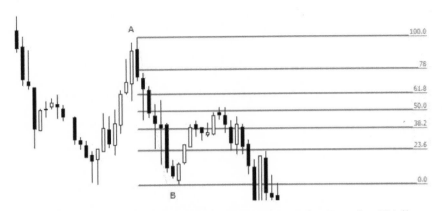

At point A there will be the 100% line and at point B – the 0% line.

In an uptrend, when you look for a long opportunity, you draw your retracement from **low (A) to high (B)**:

In such cases at point A there will be the 100% line and at point B – the 0% line.

CONCLUSION

This brings us to the end of the book.

First of all, I would personally like to congratulate you on deciding to improve your trading with my assistance on Fibonacci. If you are reading this section, you are one step closer to pushing your trading results to the next level!

By the way, if you find you have learnt something useful via this book, please leave a few kind words in the review section. I would be very grateful to you.

My Best Always!

Frank Miller

Made in the USA
Middletown, DE
12 March 2020